Back to the Garden
Learning to Trust God Again

Other works by BL Gabriel:

Day of Salvation Journal, 2012, updated 2020

What God Sees, 2014

So, What's the Plan? Charting our New Life-Path, 2019

Back to the Garden
Learning to Trust God Again

BL Gabriel

Writing is Worship LLC
2020

ISBN: 978:0:578:71048:8

First Printing: 2020; printed in the USA.

Writing is Worship LLC
PO Box 2092
Carlsbad, CA
92018

www.BLGabriel.com

Ordering Information:
For large volume discounts, please contact the publisher by emailing
writingisworship@gmail.com.

Contents

Introduction: Actors in a Screenplay 1
   Do You Want Peace? 3
   Intimacy with God Devotional (Stanley, 2016) 5

Session 1: Do We Trust God? 7
   Ultimate Trust.. 9
   Wounded Souls..19
   Surrender Prayer...37

Session 2: He is Willing, Able and He Loves Us................39
   God's Attributes 39
   Mountain Climb Exercise 47

Session 3: Shame and the Solution 51
   Brokenness and Redemption 63

Session 4: God Blesses Us..71
   God is Faithful 71
   We are the Sheep of His Pasture..............................79

Session 5: God's Promises..83
   The Two Paths Activity 83
   God Takes Care of Us 89

Appendix..95

References...97

Acknowledgements..98

Introduction: Actors in a Screenplay

Back to the Garden, Learning to Trust God Again is ideal for a 5- to 6-week (2-hour) Bible Study. It's also the perfect length for a weekend retreat. Alternatively you can meet in the comfort of your home with friends or family. Break into groups of four to eight people and take turns reading the material out loud. There is a special benefit in hearing the words spoken. Pause to answer the questions in class and then share with one another.

This book provides the framework to help you grow spiritually and emotionally if you read it and prayerfully do the workshop questions on your own. But it can transform your life if you participate in a safe community setting. Sharing our lives and our deepest thoughts with one another greatly accelerates growth. We feel heard and less alone when someone else has similar life experiences. It's incalculable how much we can learn from each other's journeys. When we share our stories of brokenness and redemption, we greatly encourage and bless others. It requires vulnerability to share, risking judgment and even rejection, but this is the ingredient needed to send a powerful blow to any lurking false shame. After all, Jesus took our shame on the cross.

Meeting in a group setting is akin to the difference between reading a screenplay and seeing the actual movie. Your classmates are the actors and this book is the screenplay. Together, the material is so much richer when processed and acted out in the setting of a safe community. And of course, God (the Holy Spirit) is the Director.

If you feel you need more help processing the workshop you may wish to review the material one-on-one with a pastor or counselor. We have included audio from actual class discussions to enrich your experience, especially if you're unable to meet in a group.

This document contains videos that can be accessed in both the ebook version and the hard copy version through *Vimeo*.

Your classmates are the actors and this book is the screenplay. God (the Holy Spirit) is the Director.

Do You Want Peace?

Video 1 (https://vimeo.com/433803712). Password is BTTG.

Do you want peace? Do you know what to do to get it?

Of course, as believers we know that Jesus is our peace. "The punishment that brought us peace was on Him, and by His wounds we are healed" (Isaiah 53:5).

Yet peace often eludes us. Are we willing to do whatever it takes to have peace in our lives? Like give up the need to have control over everything?

Jesus says "My peace I give to you" (John 14:27). But can we receive it? Or would we rather cling to our own understanding?

It's only natural that our past experiences and wounds direct us to try to have control over our lives for our own self-protection. But Jesus is now our Protector. Not only that but He is here to heal those wounds so that we can enter into a child-like faith, a deep intimacy with the Father…a relationship like no other. Do we desire that relationship and the peace it brings and to have Him front and center in our lives? And, here's the real question, do we want it more than anything else on earth?

Adam and Eve had this rich intimacy with God in the garden. They enjoyed a beautiful, unbroken relationship. They fully trusted Him for their needs until they were deceived by the devil. He made them doubt God and His goodness. What was the result? Disaster.

Today we seem to naturally trust the enemy of our souls or the old tapes that play in our heads (which he authored) thus living a life of misdirection, mistrust and sorely missed opportunities. So are we ready to get back to the garden and relearn who we can really trust?

We can have God's peace or the enemy's anxiety. Which life do we want to live?

We can have God's peace

or the enemy's anxiety.

Which life do we want to live?

Notes:

Intimacy with God Devotional (Stanley, 2016)

Play audio https://vimeo.com/463226426 or have one person read it slowly while the others close their eyes.

"Put your head down and imagine God holding you as a loving Father embracing His beloved child. You may be surprised by the emotions you feel. Hopefully, you feel secure in His overwhelming love for you. However, it is possible that you're uncomfortable and wish to push Him away because somewhere in your heart, you don't really trust Him. You may feel a sense of conviction due to some unconfessed sin. Or you may realize that you've been running away from Him all your life when all you really wanted was to feel safe in your heavenly Father's arms."

"Whatever the case, be still and allow God to deal with whatever emotions and issues arise. Do not fear. He will teach you what to do. The Father can remove any encumbrance you have to knowing Him, and He can draw you into a deeper more intimate relationship than you have ever known."

"So consider: Do you truly trust God? Are you confident that He is able to help you? Are you convinced that the Father is willing to listen to you and come to your aid? I hope you are. But if your answer to any of these questions is no, I pray that the Father will do a mighty work in your life and show you beyond a shadow of a doubt that you can place all your hope in Him. Not only is He worthy of your trust; He also loves you unconditionally and wants to show you the extraordinary life He created you for. So spend some time in prayer today and allow Him to reveal to you who He really is."

Notes:

Session 1: Do We Trust God?

Do you trust that the chair you are sitting in will hold you up? Why? Did you do an engineering analysis of its ability to be used safely? Not likely. You simply had no apparent reason not to trust the chair. You didn't spy any cracks in the wood. The legs didn't wobble as you began to sit in it so you automatically trusted because chairs in the past have held you up just fine. After all, that is a chair's purpose and the manufacturers would certainly not sell many if they did not fulfill their intended purpose.

This analogy brings us to an infinitely more important question. Do you trust God in the good times? How about in the hard times? Why? Why not? Jeremiah outlines the benefits of trusting.

"Blessed is the man who trusts in the LORD, and whose hope is the LORD. For he shall be like a tree planted by the waters, which spreads out its roots by the river, and will not fear when heat comes; but its leaf will be green, and will not be anxious in the year of drought, nor will cease from yielding fruit."
Jeremiah 17:7-8

Do you trust God in the good times?
How about in the hard times?

Notes:

Meditate on the many benefits of trusting God in Jeremiah 17:7-8 in the space provided below:

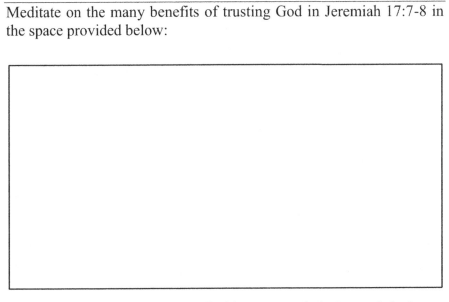

The evidence that we can trust God is so overwhelming and the benefits so great that it's worth taking a much closer look. First and foremost, the evidence is from a higher source than any chair analysis ever conducted. The Source is God Himself.

So why don't we trust God in every aspect of our lives? One or both of the following statements is likely true:

- We don't believe He is who He says He is.

- We don't believe we are who He says we are.

Ultimate Trust

Let's start with the end goal.

What does it look like to trust God?

It doesn't look like the following story. A guy was boasting to the old southern preacher, J. Vernon McGee. He said he had so much trust in God that if his time on earth was not up, he could walk straight into heavy traffic and be completely unscathed. The old preacher, without

Notes:

missing a beat, told him *"If you walk into heavy traffic, your time is up today!"*

God's promises ultimately lead to peace and rest. The scriptures below show that God's promises teach us we can trust God, and then (and only then) can we fully experience His benefits. Peace and rest follow trusting. Seems pretty simple, eh?

"For all the **promises** of God in Him are Yes, and in Him Amen, to the glory of God through us." 2 Cor. 1:20

"Trust in the LORD with all your heart, and
lean not on your own understanding." Prov. 3:5

"Bless the LORD, O my soul, and forget not all His **benefits**."
Psalm 103:2

"These things I have spoken to you, that
in Me you may have **peace**." John 16:33

"Come to Me, all you who labor and are heavy laden, and
I will give you **rest**." Matthew 11:28

Ah, what a blessed life trusting God can give us! Peace follows trust.

Of course, we have a key role to play in promoting faith in our lives. Proverbs 24:3a says "through wisdom a house is built." So we can be builders of our lives or we can tear down our lives with destructive thoughts that lead to discouragement. If we don't trust God, peace and rest won't ensue. We can build or we can self-sabotage. It's a daily, even moment by moment, choice.

Notes:

Peace and rest
Experience benefits
Trust God
God's promises
Jesus, the Rock

The Bible says repeatedly that the righteous will not be greatly shaken, but only if we remember to stand on the solid Rock.

How often we forget God and revert to standing on sinking sand?!

We sing the song *"I will build my life upon your love; it is a firm foundation. I will put my trust in You alone and I will not be shaken"* (Bethel Music). Jesus is our foundation upon which to build. He is never shaken, so if we stand on His promises we have a firm and lasting foundation.

"The wise woman builds her house, but the foolish pulls it down with her hands."
Proverbs 14:1

Notes:

"But everyone who hears these sayings of Mine,
and does not do them, will be like
a foolish man who built his house on the sand." Matthew 7:26

"Trust in the LORD forever, for the LORD,
the LORD himself, is the Rock eternal." Isaiah 26:4.

"Surely he will never be shaken; the righteous will be in
everlasting remembrance. He will not be afraid of evil tidings;
his heart is steadfast, trusting in the LORD." Ps. 112:6-7

"He only is my rock and my salvation; He is my defense;
I shall not be greatly moved." Psalm 62:2

The fact that the righteous are not shaken is not because adversity does not come into their lives, but because they trust God *in spite of* difficult circumstances. Therefore, they are not greatly shaken by them.

Holley Gerth (2014) in her highly recommended book *You're Going to Be Okay* has a very useful thoughts quiz.

This simple quiz can change our thoughts and our very lives if employed regularly!

"For as he thinks in his heart, so is he." Proverbs 23:7

Notes:

Thoughts Quiz

What does this thought bring? (Check the boxes that apply.)

☐ Love	☐ Isolation
☐ Joy	☐ Depression
☐ Peace	☐ Anxiety
☐ Patience	☐ Striving
☐ Kindness	☐ Condemnation
☐ Goodness	☐ Shame
☐ Faithfulness	☐ Doubt
☐ Gentleness	☐ Harshness
☐ Self-control	☐ Indulgence

If our thoughts lead to the right side, it is not from God. Rather, we believe lies and are therefore most certainly not building up our lives. Note that the words on the right are essentially opposites of each of the fruits of God's Holy Spirit.

On the left side are the fruits of the Holy Spirit that has His residence in us! Holley asserts that the left side is checked if the thought aligns with scripture and is of God. Let's stick to the fruitful side!

Below are some examples:

God loves me therefore I'm safe (promotes love and peace).

I can't do this trial anymore (promotes depression and anxiety).

This trial is hard but I know God is bringing good through it (promotes patience and peace).

Notes:

Wounded Souls

Video 2 (https://vimeo.com/454566409).

So, what gets in the way of ultimate trust and the benefits that follow? Pain from past experiences can block our ability to trust God. These inner wounds form false beliefs that get between our firm foundation and the truth of God and this thwarts trust because we do not believe His promises. The result is our actions and reactions to circumstances in life are vastly altered.

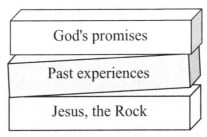

If we find ourselves "shaken" every time life feels out of our control, this is a good indicator that we do not trust God and His promises but rather our old false beliefs (aka lies). Many of us form these beliefs before the truth of God has a chance to take hold in our lives.

It may be that we learned early in life and firmly believe we have to take care of ourselves because no one else will and/or no one else can be trusted to do so. In this scenario, when difficult circumstances come that overwhelm us, our first response is fear and the familiar feeling that pain must be endured alone. But we are not alone.

So our challenge is to identify the inner wounds that drive our false beliefs and bring pain to ourselves and others. If we allow God to root out the underlying cause, we can become who He intended us to be.

Connected. Whole. Peaceful. Loving. Free.

If not, we will continue to believe the lies from the hidden wounds of our soul that speak falsely who we are not.

Not good enough. Not worthy. Not OK. Not lovable. Not deserving.

If we allow God to root out the underlying cause of our
pain, we can become who He intended us to be.

Connected. Whole. Peaceful. Loving.

If not, we will continue to believe the lies
from the hidden wounds of our soul
that speak falsely who we are not.

Not good enough. Not worthy. Not OK. Not lovable.

Notes:

"Search me, O God, and know my heart; try me, and know my anxieties; and see if there is any wicked (*hurtful*) way in me, and lead me in the way everlasting." Psalm 139:23-24

"Know the God of your Father, and serve Him with a loyal heart and with a willing mind; for the Lord searches all hearts and understands all the intent of the thoughts. If you seek Him, He will be found by you." 1 Chronicles 28:9

The purpose of this study is to bring about awareness so that at the point our faith is tested we can choose to focus on the truth about God and who we are in Christ. Then, instead of fear, we can look to Him who can handle everything. In this way we can more fully drink in His word and the promises it brings. As we shed our vows arising from inner pain and allow God to bring healing to the past experiences, God's Word will come more alive than ever in our lives, resulting in increased trust and the ensuing rest and peace that He promises.

"Tis so sweet to trust in Jesus. Just to take him at his word."
Louisa Stead (1882)

On the other hand, if we don't trust when difficult circumstances come, we'll have fear and despair in our heart and mind all the time. Charles Stanley (2005) says *"Could anything feel more disconcerting or frightening than having to face a terrible trial all by yourself? God tells us that those who know Him never have to worry about that."*

Yet, many of us live as though we do. At these times, our experience may follow a pattern similar to the graphic shown below. Although there is a firm foundation, the past experiences unbalance our lives and we are shaken.

As we shed our vows arising from inner pain and allow God to bring healing to the past experiences, God's Word will come more alive than ever in our lives, resulting in increased trust and the ensuing rest and peace that He promises.

Notes:

It's not a pretty picture:

Jesus: We have Jesus as our firm foundation upon which we can stand, but do we stand?

Past experiences: Past wounds affect our thoughts, beliefs and decisions and often derail us.

God's promises: God's promises tell us the truth about God and ourselves.

Difficult circumstances: Circumstances challenge us and show us what we really believe. We often doubt God's word.

Fear: Fear is a familiar feeling that beckons us to trust it instead of God. We think fear will help to protect us somehow.

Not trusting God: We are shaken because we trust lies and this blocks God's truth because faith and fear cannot co-exist.

No peace: Peace eludes us because we are not believing the truth (and the truth will set us free). First we must be anxious for nothing; it is then that peace is promised (Philippians 4:6-7).

Despair: Loss of hope is the end result.

Notes:

We may have times of trusting and victory but it is not as consistent as we would like. Situations trigger fear in us. If we feel emotionally "hysterical" it may be related to a lie associated with something "historical" in our lives that has caused us great pain. We are in need of healing in this area to replace the lie with God's truth. God wants to heal our emotional pain if we are willing to face it and let Him do the rest. While facing and feeling pain is incredibly hard, living with it unresolved is ultimately the more difficult path both on ourselves and on our relationships. Meditate on the rich verses below.

"He heals the brokenhearted and binds up their wounds."
Psalm 147:3

"A bruised reed He will not break." Isaiah 42:3a

"Remove falsehood and lies far from me." Proverbs 30:8a

Even the strongest of us is limited and therefore needs God's help whether we realize it or not. A comedy movie had a scene with a guy in danger of drowning. He was lost and alone, swimming way out at sea. He said *"God I'll give you the next 50 years of my life if you rescue me!"* As he drifted and could actually begin to see the vague outline of the shoreline, he was still in trouble but felt more hopeful and so he said *"God I'll give you 5 years of my life!"* Later, when he began to feel bottom and was nearly safely ashore he said *"God, I got this!"* Often, rather than being thankful that God does indeed rescue us, we try to do it on our own and claim self-sufficiency. This gives us a sense of security, albeit false. At least until the next trial...

If we are feeling helpless and shaken much of the time, we are forgetting or not truly grasping that God is in control. Since our primary

Notes:

caregivers may have been absent or dysfunctional or even abusive in some capacity, we set out to take care of ourselves and ultimately find that we are sorely lacking. We do not fully believe the truth that God is trustworthy and that He deems us worthy through Jesus and wants to tenderly care for us, His children. The truth is we are not alone.

There was a story about how a dog rescuer operates. She tries not to overwhelm the scared, loose dog by running towards it. Rather she woos it gently by outstretching her hand and letting the pup come to her. In the same way, God invites us into a relationship with Him. He doesn't demand that we come. He gently pursues us.

This is similar to the love story told in the Bible in the book of Hosea. Hosea woos his wayward wife, Gomer, illustrating how God draws Israel (and us) to Himself.

"I drew them with gentle cords, with bands of love, And I was to them as those who take the yoke from their neck.
I stooped and fed them." Hosea 11:4

Edward Welch in his amazing book, *Shame Interrupted* (2012), says that God gladly invites us to a meal. If we have nothing to bring, that is the price of admission. God wants an intimate relationship with us. And He paid the ultimate price to get it. We don't have to perform to receive His love.

The exercise below will help us to root out the false messages so God's Word can begin to reign in our hearts and minds.

Notes:

Video 3 (https://vimeo.com/440736951). Password is past.

What painful past experiences are shaping your life today? Briefly record one to three experiences below.

1.

_____

2.

_____

3.

_____

What corresponding emotions are associated with each of these experiences?

1.

_____

2.

_____

3.

_____

Here is a partial list of emotions. Feel free to add your own.

unloved	inadequate	out of control	invalidated
unworthy	hopeless	controlled	not enough
insignificant	unwanted	vulnerable	rejected
alone	unsafe	unknown	fearful
worthless	insecure	abandoned	unfair
misunderstood	devalued	powerless	failure
defective	guilty	unsure	desperate
betrayed	frustrated	suspicious	used
jealous	unheard	disconnected	powerless

Notes:

What are the false messages you believe about each of these experiences?

1.

2.

3.

Common false messages are *"I'm not good enough," "I'm not OK"* or *"I'm defective,"* and *"I don't deserve to be loved."*

What does God's Word say about these false messages?

1.

2.

3.

Search the scriptures for the truth about God and the truth about you such as the following truths countering the common false messages listed above: *"God made me and I'm His," "As a child of God I never have to be ashamed,"* and *"God is love and He loves me."*

Summarize the above information in the table provided. An example is included in the table. See the Appendix for more examples.

(Note: If this exercise brings up difficult emotions you may want to consult a pastor or counselor, as needed).

Notes:

Example
Painful experience: Parents divorced
Emotions: abandoned / rejected / inadequate
False Message: I'm not good enough / I'm not safe in conflict
Truth: "He made us accepted in the Beloved." I am wrapped in Christ. (Ephesians 1:6)

Painful experience: _____

Emotions: _____

False Message: _____

Truth: _____

Painful experience: _____

Emotions: _____

False Message: _____

Truth: _____

Painful experience: _____

Emotions: _____

False Message: _____

Truth: _____

Notes:

Ask God to replace the false message with the truth of His Word. Otherwise these lies can run our lives. Thankfully, God is in the business of healing our wounded parts so He can use us for His glory.

Notes:

Surrender Prayer

Lord, all your promises are yes and amen.

My difficult circumstances do not escape your notice. Your eye is on the sparrow and I know you're watching me. Please guide me in the best path for me and for your glory.

Help me to overcome this pain and the fear and lies attached to it, Lord, and help me to rely on You to handle every aspect of my life. Thank you that, while I may not be in control of this situation, I'm not out of control either; I'm in Your control. The best place to be.

This day I surrender _____
to you (release it by tossing a leaf or flower into the water) and I look forward to seeing what you will do in your power as You heal me as only You can. Thank You that I do not have a spirit of fear but of power, love and a sound mind. In fact, You say I have the mind of Christ! Thank you for your presence forever that will never leave me.

I receive your unconditional love and everlasting peace afresh now. And, Lord, I love you back!

Show me the way forward, Lord.

Amen.

Notes:

Session 2: He is Willing, Able and He Loves Us

Of course, we must know God in order to trust Him.

Do we believe He is who He says He is?

Do we trust that God is able and willing to handle any problem that we experience?

Do we believe that He loves us...unconditionally?

God's Attributes

If we aren't sure He is willing, able and loving let's review a few of His attributes. They tell a story of a powerful God who loves and cares immensely for us.

ATTRIBUTE: God knows everything that concerns me (Omniscient)

My response: Ask Him to guide me in the best path for me and for His glory

"For You formed my inward parts; You covered me in my mother's womb. I will praise You, for I am fearfully and wonderfully made; marvelous are Your works, and that my soul knows very well. My frame was not hidden from You, when I was made in secret, and skillfully wrought in the lowest parts of the earth. Your eyes saw my substance, being yet unformed. And in Your book they all were written, the days fashioned for me, when as yet there were none of them." Psalm 139:13-16

Notes:

ATTRIBUTE: God is all powerful and capable of helping me (Omnipotent)

My response: Ask him for help and then rely on Him to answer

"Behold, I am the LORD, the God of all flesh. Is there anything too hard for Me?" Jeremiah 32:27

ATTRIBUTE: God will never leave me (Omnipresent)

My response: Have confidence in God's presence

"Be strong and of good courage, do not fear nor be afraid of them; for the LORD your God, He is the One who goes with you. He will not leave you nor forsake you." Deuteronomy 31:6

"For He Himself has said, 'I will never leave you nor forsake you.' So we may boldly say: 'The LORD is my helper; I will not fear. What can man do to me?'" Hebrews 13:5-6

ATTRIBUTE: God always acts in my best interest (Unconditional love)

My response: Love Him back!

"And we know that all things work together for good to those who love God, to those who are the called according to His purpose." Romans 8:28

"Cause me to hear Your lovingkindness in the morning, for in You do I trust; cause me to know the way in which I should walk, for I lift up my soul to You." Psalm 143:8

"And walk in love, as Christ also has loved us and given Himself for us, an offering and a sacrifice to God for a sweet-smelling aroma." Ephesians 5:2

"In this is love, not that we loved God, but that He loved us and sent His Son to be the propitiation for our sins." 1 John 4:10

Feeling insignificant?

"The very hairs of your head are all numbered."
Matthew 10:30

Notes:

Which of these attributes most challenge your current false perceptions? Are you willing to give up the false perception and embrace God's truth instead?

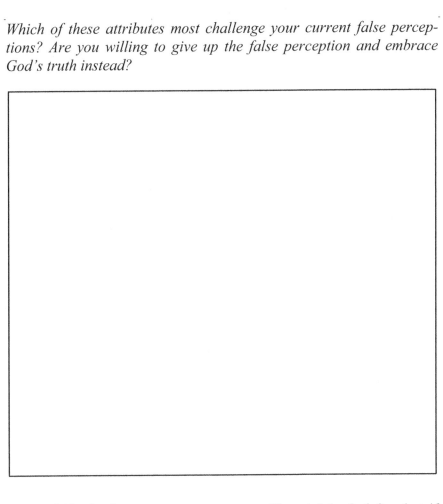

When difficult circumstances come we will certainly feel fear but if we remember who He is and who we are in Him, we can pray and ask God to change our focus to Him and His power instead of our meager personal resources. Focusing on our problems brings fear. Focusing on God brings peace. What we focus on grows.

The good news is, God is the Source and He provides the resources. We do not need to worry or count on man because if one resource dries up, the Source will provide another to care for His beloved children. Once we realize who He is and how He cares for us, peace should result.

The good news is, God is the Source and He provides the resources…if one resource dries up, the Source will provide another to care for His beloved children.

Notes:

Because our past experiences affect how we view God's promises, when difficult circumstances come we often fear (believe lies from the past) until we look to God with faith (believe the truth) and then peace returns as shown below.

If we surrender our fears, He will gladly take them and replace them with His peace and presence.

Are there any concerns not addressed by God in light of His attributes? _____

- He knows everything that concerns me

- He is all powerful

- He never leaves me

- He loves me unconditionally

Notes:

Mountain Climb Exercise

Play audio https://vimeo.com/463224828 or have a member of your group read it. Optional: play *Nothing I hold Onto* by United Pursuit.

Visualize you are walking up a mountain. The vegetation is dry and sparse, but you can see green, towering trees with flowing waterfalls near the peak.

The terrain is slowly rising and the trail is not too rigorous so you are barely breaking a sweat. You come upon a gift in the road which you know is for you. You stop to pick it up.

What is the gift?

_____

After a long while the trail gets narrower and you encounter boulders which you choose to successfully go around.

Further on, the trail is steeply winding and difficult; you look for a foothold and a handhold and you are somehow able to propel yourself past a rather large obstacle. You wipe the sweat off your brow.

What is the obstacle?

_____

Relieved, you look up only to see there is a long stretch of switchbacks yet to traverse in order to reach the top. Although weary, you soldier on.

Finally, you come around a bend where you are delighted to find a running stream. Jesus is sitting on a rock, apparently

Notes:

waiting just for you. You gladly take a drink from the sparkling water and sit down to rest with Him. What do you want to ask Him?

_____

What is His response?

_____

_____

Notes:

Session 3: Shame and the Solution

Sometimes we hold onto our fears and pain for reasons that elude and frustrate us. So, what more do we want? If we know He is willing and able and loving, then do we want the assurance that we are worth loving? Worth knowing? Worth having Him flex His power to help us?

He says, as His children, we are worth saving so He sent His Son to do just that.

Still, nagging doubts often come. If I'm not good enough, why on earth would He consider me deserving of His help, presence, love or care?

Brene Brown is a researcher who has done extensive work on shame and vulnerability. She defines shame as:

> *"The intensely painful feeling that we are flawed and therefore unworthy of love and belonging."*

Shame shapes everything without our even knowing it. It depends on us buying into the belief that we are alone. In order to survive, shame requires *secrecy, silence and judgment.*

Shame can negate the reception of God's blessings in our lives, at least on an emotional level and of course our emotions fuel our behavior and ultimately our life direction.

Shame has the tendency to make us want to hide and self-protect. And not asking for help because we don't think we will get it (much less deserve it) only assures us of further isolation and living in shame. It can become an endless cycle.

Notes:

What are you hiding from others? What do you fear would happen if they found out? Is that true? Write or draw your response below.

Sometimes we don't want to "bother" people when we need something. But God is different! He wants us to ask. He wants to help us. He wants to be with us. We are most definitely not alone. We can trust God instead of our self-protecting and self-defeating strategies (Welch, 2012).

What messages about yourself did you receive from either your family or your peers during your childhood that still impact you today?

Back to the Garden, Learning to Trust God Again

Notes:

Do you believe and receive God's promises? Which ones are you not trusting are yours (salvation, love, acceptance, blessing, belonging, intimacy, and power, to name a few)? Why do you think that is the case? Refer back to the table in Session 1 for possible clues.

Let's address an earlier question: *Do we believe we are who He says we are?*

The story of Gideon in Judges 6 finds God calling Gideon *mighty*. Gideon must have looked behind him and squeaked, "*Who, me*?" He saw himself as weak and little.

"The Angel of the LORD...said to him 'The LORD is with you, you mighty man of valor.'" Judges 6:11-12.

"So he said to Him, "O my Lord, how can I save Israel? Indeed my clan is the weakest in Manasseh, and I am the least in my father's house." Judges 6:15

Charles Stanley (2005) says *"When we believe God and not ourselves we become what He says we are."* Gideon obeyed and proved God right. The secret to success is the presence of God!

"When we believe God and
not ourselves, we become
what He says we are."

Charles Stanley

Notes:

It's also important to remember that we have an adversary of the faith that wants to kill, steal and destroy (see John 10:10). The enemy of our souls is a skilled deceiver.

A pastor once said "*fish don't bite hooks.*" This refers to how the enemy wraps the hooks in some desirable bait. Instead of telling you "*You should tell a lie to get your way,*" he'll say "*You deserve to be happy!*" And we are more likely to take the bait when the hook is carefully wrapped that way. Once the hook goes in deep it is difficult to get out!

In the garden of Eden, the enemy lied and twisted the truth so that Adam and Eve were greatly deceived. What was the result of them believing his lies? Shame.

"I heard Your voice in the garden, and I was afraid because I was naked; and I hid myself." Genesis 3:10

There is a downward spiral that occurs when shame is in our lives as shown below both in words and graphically.

Past Shame: When shame is part of our foundation, it greatly affects how or if we receive God's promises in our lives. For example, *"I don't deserve"* comes to mind often.

God's Promises: His promises are ours for the taking but become murky when seen and skewed through the filter of past shame.

Isolation: Shame breeds isolation and disconnection which only serve to keep us in a place of shame.

Notes:

Fear: Fear comes because we are not abiding in God's love and truth. "There is no fear in love; but perfect love casts out fear" (1 John 4:18).

Believe lies: We are set up to believe lies because of our tendency to shame ourselves.

Can't receive blessings: We can't receive blessings because we don't feel we deserve anything.

Despair: The result is despair (loss of hope).

Brene Brown says shame breeds *fear, blame and disconnection*. But if we share our shameful experience with someone and we receive empathy the shame will disappear. Wow.

Activity: Play Brown video on Shame and Empathy 8:38 minutes. (https://www.youtube.com/watch?v=qQiFfA7KfF0)

Notes:

Ms. Brown says that vulnerability will eliminate shame but we are afraid to be vulnerable because we fear it will cause disconnection. In a society so dependent on belonging and fitting in this is a huge risk. However, we're wired to tell our stories, so we must take the risk or stay in shame.

Are you comfortable sharing an experience that caused you to feel shame? The empathy you receive will begin to heal the emotions from that experience.

God, thank you for taking my shame, including:

Notes:

Activity: Now take this shame list from the previous page and throw it in the fireplace or into the trash can or bury it in the garden for the worms to digest where it belongs!

Many people see God using their mess to become their message to help others. What a good God! Who can we encourage today with our story of redemption?

"You will cast all our sins into the depths of the sea."
Micah 7:19

I think it was Corrie Ten Boom who first said God has cast our sins into the sea and posted a "No Fishing" sign!

"And all the wickedness in the world that man may do or think is no more to the mercy of God than a live coal dropped in the sea."

William Langland

Brokenness and Redemption

We were born to tell our stories. Brene Brown says that connection is the "essence of the human experience."

Notes:

If you met someone you felt was safe to share with and they asked "So, what's your story?" what would you tell them? Write a brief description of what first comes to mind.

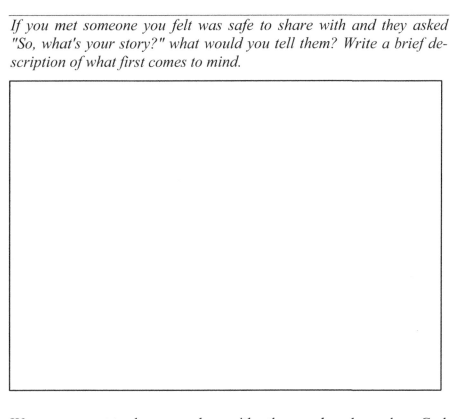

We were meant to share ourselves with others and explore where God is leading us. But when shame came it silenced us to secrecy because it caused us to believe lies about ourselves and therefore hide our beautiful stories of brokenness and redemption. We hide ourselves from connection to avoid the pain of judgment and rejection.

But the cross redeems us and tells a very different story. All shame is gone. G-O-N-E.

This includes shame for the sins we have committed and shame for the sins others have committed against us (so we can forgive them). The scriptures confirm that God has taken away our shame.

Can we agree with God, surrender the lies of shame, and gratefully receive God's love and truth instead?

Notes:

Dan Allender (2005) says God is the Author of our stories and we are the co-authors. He will show us how to follow Him into the future He has planned for us. Our part is to participate and engage in the process and not let (false) shame silence us. Jesus already paid the price in full.

God's promises are ours. Jesus took our shame. We can believe and embrace the truth. We can receive God's blessings because He offers them freely! Drink in the true words below from scripture.

"The punishment that brought us **peace** was on Him, and by His wounds we are **healed**." Isaiah 53:5

"Instead of your shame you shall have **double honor**, and instead of confusion they shall rejoice in their portion. Therefore in their land they shall possess double; everlasting joy shall be theirs." Isaiah 61:7

"To the praise of the glory of His grace, by which He made us **accepted** in the Beloved." Ephesians 1:6

"And let us consider one another in order to stir up love and good works, not forsaking the **assembling of ourselves together**, as is the manner of some, but exhorting one another, and so much the more as you see the Day approaching." Hebrews 10:24-25

"Do not be afraid. Only **believe**." Mark 5:36

"Who has blessed us with every spiritual **blessing** in the heavenly places in Christ." Ephesians 1:3

Notes:

And when we receive God's blessings, we can bless others! Graphically, it looks like this:

God's promises: We are now free to receive God's promises as ours.
Jesus took our shame: With shame gone we can once again connect with others without the fear of judgment.
Loved and accepted: We are not flawed but loved and accepted through grace.
Belong: We are not isolated but we belong to a community of believers.
Believe the truth: We can see and believe the truth without blocks.
Receive blessings: We can receive blessings as thankful children of God who are blessed forever. Notice in God's Kingdom it is believe and then receive.

We are now engaged in following the Author of our stories in hopeful anticipation of the future. The cross is proof that we can trust God with our stories and our lives. Jesus said "*It is finished.*" And it is. He is ours and we are His.

> Then you will know that I am the LORD. For they shall
> **not be ashamed** who wait for Me. Isaiah 49:23b

The cross is proof that
we can trust God. He is
ours and we are His.

Notes:

Session 4: God Blesses Us

Because of who He is and whose we are, God's plan is to bless us. Think about that a minute. The God of the universe wants to bless _____ (insert your name). This is amazing news!

"Every good gift and every perfect gift is from above, and comes down from the Father of lights, with whom there is no variation or shadow of turning." James 1:17

"Or what man is there among you who, if his son asks for bread, will give him a stone? Or if he asks for a fish, will he give him a serpent? If you then, being evil, know how to give good gifts to your children, how much more will your Father who is in heaven give good things to those who ask Him!" Matt. 7:9-11

What's the best gift you have ever received? Why was it the best?

God is Faithful

We talked about chairs in an earlier session. When we go to sit down, we usually put our trust in the chair because chairs in the past have held us up just fine. But if you have ever had a chair let you down, you may be a bit more cautious. I remember my grandmother sitting

Notes:

in one of those beach chairs that were great because we could re-strip them rather than replace the whole chair. But the chair strips had rotted, unbeknownst to her, and she fell right through it onto the concrete patio next to our pool! She laughed but I'm sure she was embarrassed. She may have been inclined to test beach chairs before sitting down for a while after that! I know I did.

In the same way, we may not trust God because we live in a world where hard things happen to people and we have experienced difficult days ourselves. We say *"I just don't understand God's ways!"* But it's those very trials that He uses to teach us we can trust Him. Charles Stanley says when we need to rely on God, it's then that we receive the abundant life that He intended to give us. But when we rely only on ourselves, we receive the limited life we can provide. Now that is something to ponder!

"For as the heavens are higher than the earth, so are My ways higher than your ways, and My thoughts than your thoughts." Isaiah 55:9

"Trust in the LORD with all your heart, and lean not on your own understanding; in all your ways acknowledge Him, and He shall direct your paths. Do not be wise in your own eyes; fear the LORD and depart from evil. It will be health to your flesh, and strength to your bones." Proverbs 3: 5-8

Still, sometimes the world doesn't seem safe. Doubt creeps in.

"Do not be afraid, only believe." Mark 5:36

Notes:

"These things I have spoken to you, that in Me you may have peace. In the world you will have tribulation; but be of good cheer, I have overcome the world." John 16:32-33

God assures us through His word that we are His. We are loved and we belong to Him.

"I have called you by name. You are Mine." Isaiah 43:1

What do you want to ask or tell God about the verses above? Do you believe God's thoughts are higher than your thoughts? Are you sometimes tempted to be wise in your own eyes? Does it comfort you that God says He has called you by name?

Charles Stanley (2005) says *"Adversity is a bridge to a deeper relationship with God."* Do we want that deeper relationship?

A favorite line from the poem, *The Hound of Heaven* by Francis Thompson, appears to confirm this thought.

"Is my gloom, after all, shade of His hand outstretched caressingly?"

It would seem that God uses whatever works to draw us and lead us to the abundant life He has planned all along. Why? Because He loves us.

Hannah Whitall Smith in her book *The God of All Comfort* quotes from Isaiah 28:15 and 17 "For we have made lies our refuge, and un-

Back to the Garden, Learning to Trust God Again

Notes:

der falsehood we have hidden ourselves…the Lord will sweep away the refuge of lies and cause the waters to overflow the hiding place." Smith encourages us by saying although it's God's wrath against the refuge of lies, it is not His wrath against us but rather it's His love that does this in order to deliver us from what can be shaken so that only those things which cannot be shaken remain.

The truth is, if we look carefully, God gives us what we need in times of trial, and then some. Can we receive it?

"For God has not given us a spirit of fear,
but of power and of love and a sound mind." 2 Timothy 1:7

"The thief does not come except to steal, and to kill, and to destroy. I have come that they may have life, and that they may have it more abundantly." John 10:10

We must not let our past difficult experiences negate our past amazing experiences with God. But rather see how He met us and strengthened us, carrying us through to the other side.

Do you believe God wants to give you abundant life? Why or why not? What do you think "abundant" means?

Notes:

Do you recall a time when God totally came through for you? Do you recall a time when He didn't?

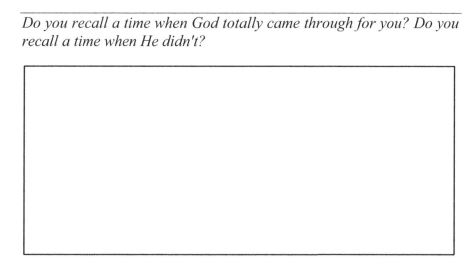

The many times He has come through for us (some we don't even know about!) far outweigh the disappointing times. Researchers say our brains naturally tend to focus on the negative experiences more. So we have to remind ourselves of His tender care throughout the years. Record these memories in a journal for safekeeping and reference. If helpful, create a timeline of significant events in your life.

We can have faith; we can believe because He has been and will be faithful. Until heaven, then forever.

"When you go out to battle against your enemies, and see horses and chariots and people more numerous than you, do not be afraid of them; for the LORD your God is with you, who brought you up from the land of Egypt." Deuteronomy 20:1

We are the Sheep of His Pasture

God refers to us as sheep. Sheep need a lot of assistance in life. They are not very smart. So we can count on Him understanding that we need help too. We don't need to do it all ourselves. We're not the only one responsible to take care of ourselves. We can take care of what is in our sphere of ability. Then God takes over. But are we letting Him take over?

If you can trust God for anything, you can trust God for everything!

Notes:

"Come to Me, all you who labor and are heavy laden, and
I will give you rest." Matthew 11:28

After all God has said and done, it's still hard for some of us to grasp
that He is responsible to take care of His children. Especially when
we grew up feeling we are responsible for everything! But a good Father cares for his children. And He is the very best.

*Are you an overly responsible person? Is there one way you can let
God be God? Does God really say He is responsible for taking care
of us?* Search for and record scriptures regarding this statement.

Video 4 (https://vimeo.com/440476996). Password is easybutton.

Notes:

Session 5: God's Promises

The Two Paths Activity

Video 5 (https://vimeo.com/436276693). Password is twopaths.

God's promises are filtered through our past experiences. When difficult circumstances come, fear is often our first response. There are two paths we can take when fear beckons. Start at the bottom of the page and work your way up in each path starting with the left path.

What false assumptions can you discard?

What are you hoping for today?

What do you need?

What is the reason for your peace?

What are you feeling and believing?

What promise of God are you believing?

Why worry? (i.e., how does worry protect you?)

What is God's response to your fear?

Worry and analyze (i.e., me in control)

Trust God (i.e., God in control)

START HERE

When difficult circumstances come we filter them through our experiential and scriptural beliefs. Let's ask ourselves what we are afraid of today and what is the source of our fear? Which path do we live on most of the time? Which path do we want to live on?

Notes:

Additionally, when fear comes what we do with it is key.

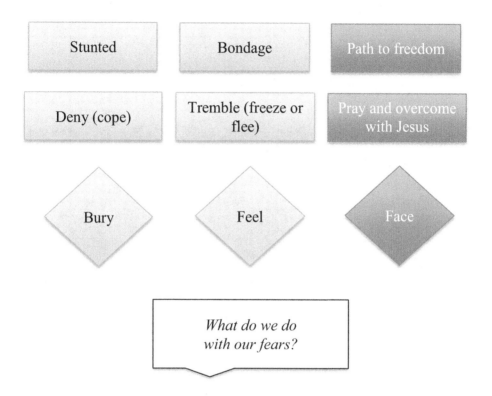

The truth is sometimes we trust God for heaven but not for aspects of life in which we have been wounded. So God in His mercy helps us to work on the very areas where we need to trust Him more and then His benefits and peace will come. God is good. As we realize we belong to Him, we will learn to trust Him more consistently. Trust breeds trust. With us in control, life is stressful; with God in control, life can be peaceful.

Of course, learning to trust is a process, and it is usually uncomfortable because of past wounds. But Jesus gave 100% of Himself for us. Therefore, we can (humbly) receive 100% of the benefits that His sacrifice brings.

An example of partial belief is shown in the following graphic.

Notes:

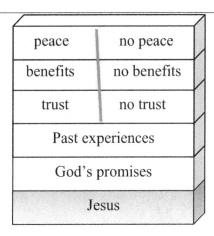

If we trust God 50% of the time, then 50% of the time we are not living with benefits and peace. What is the hardest area for you to trust?

"Blessed be the Lord, who daily loads us with benefits."
Psalm 68:19

Fill in God's promise on the line below. Add your own vertical lines to show the percentage of current trust in this area.

peace	no peace
benefits	no benefits
trust	no trust
God's promise: _____	
Jesus	

Video 6 (https://vimeo.com/440474387). Password is 100%.

Notes:

Why is it hard to trust in this area? Listen for the Holy Spirit's response. Refer back to the table in Session 1 for clues.

Awareness is the path to change! Keep this chart handy and refer to it as a reminder of the goal of accepting 100% of God's benefits.

God Takes Care of Us

God isn't surprised by our needs. That's a huge relief. Brene Brown says *"Courage is asking for what you need."* We need to first recognize our needs. We can't change what we don't see.

What do you need? (i.e., rest, belonging, hope, love, affirmation, touch, fun, understanding, loyalty, security, significance, etc.)

Notes:

We often don't get our emotional needs fully met by our primary caregivers growing up which can suggest to us that we are not valuable. To combat this feeling we may:

☐ Try not to have needs (i.e., claim self-sufficiency);
☐ Believe we don't deserve getting our needs met if we did have them (i.e., hide); or
☐ Don't realize we even have needs (i.e., live in denial).

But God wants us to ask Him for what we need!

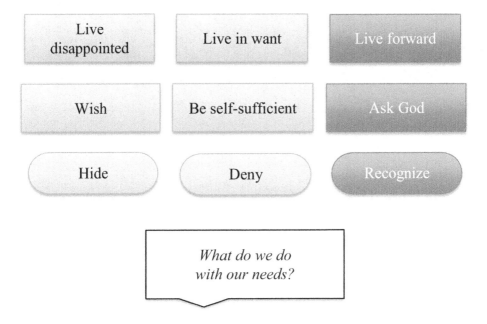

God knows our past hurts impede us so He came to meet our deepest needs. Remember, God is different from people, including:

- God values and understands us and our needs better than we understand ourselves.
- God is able when we're not (which is often).

Notes:

- God is here when others have let us down (which is sometimes).
- God loves like no one else because He is Love!

It all comes down to trusting God. We only feel that we belong, are loved and are safe if we are trusting God as our unshakable Source. Can we stop trying to manage our situation and invite Him to handle it?

This journey is a process and God is patient with us. He knows our human frailty. We are a royal work in progress and He will give us everything we need to succeed (Philippians 1:6; 4:13).

So, how do we know we can trust God? Two simple, yet profound statements are true:
- He is willing, able, and He loves us, and
- We are His.

I am His and He is Mine
(George Robinson, 1876)
"Things that once were wild alarms
cannot now disturb my rest,
clothed in everlasting arms,
pillowed on His loving breast;
Oh, to lie forever here,
doubt and care and self resign,
while He whispers in my ear
I am His, and He is mine."

"Thanks be to God for His indescribable gift!"
2 Corinthians 9:15

Appendix

Below are possible examples from Session 1. Each individual may have differing emotions, messages and truth unique to them and their life. This is provided just to get our juices flowing!

Painful experience: Parents divorced
Emotions: abandoned / rejected
False Message: I'm not good enough / I'm not safe in conflict
Truth: "I am fully accepted in the beloved," I am wrapped in Christ. (Ephesians 1:6)

Painful experience: Alcoholic parent
Emotions: stoic / unsafe / out of control / vulnerable
False Message: I'm not safe so I need to be hyper vigilant / anxious
Truth: God is in control and He loves me and therefore I am safe. "He who dwells in the secret place of the Most High shall abide under the shadow of the Almighty." (Psalm 91)

Painful experience: Neglected by caregivers
Emotions: hurt / alone / unwanted / defective
False Message: unlovable / not worthy of love
Truth: "I have loved you with an everlasting love." (Jeremiah 31:3)

Painful experience: Sibling rivalry
Emotions: ignored / inadequate
False Message: failure / don't measure up / don't deserve
Truth: "I have called you by name. You are Mine." (Isaiah 43:1)

Painful experience: Lied to by someone important
Emotions: suspicious / not trusting / alone
False Message: No one is trustworthy / I'm not safe
Truth: "The fear of man is a snare, but whoever trusts in the LORD shall be safe." (Proverbs 29:25)

References

Allender, Dan. 2005. *To Be Told. God Invites You to Co-author Your Future.* Waterbrook Press.

Brown, Brene. 2019. Internet research, Ted Talks and videos. Public Domain. https://www.youtube.com/watch?v=qQiFfA7KfF0

Gerth, Holly. 2014. *You're Going to be Okay. Encouraging Truth your Heart Needs to Hear, Especially on the Hard Days. Thoughts Quiz excerpted. Used by permission of Revell, a Division of Baker Publishing Group.*

Robinson, George. 1876. *I am His and He is Mine.* Public Domain.

Smith, Hannah Whitall. 1956. *The God of All Comfort.* Moody Publishers.

Stanley, Charles. 2005. Life Principles Bible. Thomas Nelson Publishing.

Stanley, Charles F. Copyright 2016 by Charles F. Stanley. *WISDOM FROM ABOVE.* Reprinted with the permission of Howard Books, a division of Simon & Schuster Inc. All rights reserved.

Stead, Louisa, 1882. *'Tis So Sweet to Trust in Jesus.* Public Domain.
Thompson, Francis. 1890. *The Hound of Heaven.* Public Domain.

Welch, Edward. *Shame Interrupted. How God Lifts the Pain of Worthlessness and Rejection.* 2012.

Acknowledgements

Thanks to my wonderful "actors" that tested out this material with me and allowed God to work as only He can. Special thanks for your vulnerability in sharing yourselves with our readers in the videos. You know God and you know who you are in Him.

And thanks be to God for his indescribable gift!